TRANSFORMING!
CHEMICAL ENERGY

Emma Carlson Berne

PowerKiDS
press.

New York

Published in 2013 by The Rosen Publishing Group, Inc.
29 East 21st Street, New York, NY 10010

First Edition

Editor: Jennifer Way
Book Design: Andrew Povolny

Photo Credits: Cover Stocktrek/Photodisc/Getty Images; pp. 4–5 Elena Elisseeva/Shutterstock.com; p. 6 Jupiterimages/Brand X Pictures/Thinkstock; p. 7 Tom Grill/The Image Bank/Getty Images; p. 8 Curve/The Agenc Collection/Getty Images; p. 9 Science & Society Picture Library/SSPL/Getty Images; p. 10 Hemera/Thinkstock; p 11 Time & Life Pictures/Getty Images; p. 12 Alexa Miller/Photodisc/Getty Images; p. 13 (top) Dave King/Dorling Kindersley/Getty Images; p. 13 (bottom) Geri Lavrov/Flickr/Getty Images; p. 14 IS Stock/Valueline/Thinkstock; p. 15 vlahuta/Shutterstock.com; p. 16 Greg Dale/National Geographic/Getty Images; p. 17 Brian Sytnyk/ Photographer's Choice/Getty Images; p. 18 Gary Whitton/Shutterstock.com; p. 19 iStockphoto/Thinkstock; p. 20 Sam Bloomberg-Rissman/Flickr/Getty Images; p. 21 (top) altafulla/Shutterstock.com; p. 21 (bottom) Bloomberg/ Getty Images; p. 22 Argonne National Laboratory/Photo Researchers/Getty Images.

Library of Congress Cataloging-in-Publication Data
Berne, Emma Carlson.
 Transforming! : chemical energy / by Emma Carlson Berne. — 1st ed.
    p. cm. — (Energy everywhere)
Includes index.
 ISBN 978-1-4488-9652-3 (library binding) — ISBN 978-1-4488-9762-9 (pbk.) —
 ISBN 978-1-4488-9763-6 (6-pack)
 1. Reactivity (Chemistry)—Juvenile literature. 2. Chemical kinetics—Juvenile literature. I. Title.
 QD501.B456 2013
 541'.394—dc23

                                  2012022947

Manufactured in the United States of America

CPSIA Compliance Information: Batch #W13PK4: For Further Information contact Rosen Publishing, New York, New York at 1-800-237-9932

CONTENTS

WHAT IS CHEMICAL ENERGY?

Look at a tree. If you can see sunlight shining on its leaves, you are seeing an example of **chemical** energy. Every time your stomach digests your lunch, you are experiencing chemical energy. Every time you stare into the flames of a campfire, you are watching chemical energy!

Energy is the ability of a system to do work. Our world has many different kinds of energy. Sound, electricity, light, and heat are a few examples. Chemical energy is the energy caused by chemical **reactions**. This book will talk about chemical energy and explore how it works.

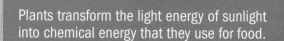

Plants transform the light energy of sunlight into chemical energy that they use for food.

CHEMICALS AND MATTER

Everything on Earth is made of **matter**. Matter is anything that takes up space and has weight. A rock is made of matter. A speck of dust is matter, too.

Matter is made up of tiny bits called **particles**. Particles are joined together in another, slightly larger form called an atom. The atoms **bond**, or are held together, in different shapes. These shapes are called **molecules**.

The soccer ball you kick and the field you play on are made of matter. You are made of matter, too.

The metal gold is a chemical that is made up of only gold atoms. These kinds of chemicals are called elements.

An arrangement of molecules forms a chemical. When molecules are joined in certain ways, they can form water, a tree, a nail, or a slice of bread. Molecules form everything in our world, including you!

BREAKING BONDS

Chemicals form bonds, and the bonds they form can be changed when they react with other chemicals. In a chemical reaction, bonds are either being formed or broken. This forming or breaking of a bond is what causes chemical energy to be released.

When you study chemistry, you are studying the properties of different chemicals. You also learn about how bonds form and break.

JAMES JOULE

James Joule was an English scientist who lived from 1818 until 1889. He studied the relationships between different forms of energy. His work helped develop the scientific laws that describe how energy works. The unit of measuring energy called the joule is named for him.

James Joule

For instance, the chemicals that make up a slice of bread have energy stored in them. When you eat and digest the bread, your stomach breaks down the chemical bonds in the bread. The energy stored in those bonds is released. Your body uses this energy to fuel itself.

STORING ENERGY

Chemical energy is stored in the bonds between chemicals. Plants, for instance, store chemical energy. They turn light from the Sun into chemical energy that feeds the plant. This same stored chemical energy is what an animal uses when it eats that plant.

Fossil fuels, such as coal, store chemical energy as well. When we burn the fossil fuels, the energy in their bonds is broken and released. Batteries store chemical energy, too. When we attach a battery to a radio, for example, the bonds stored within the battery are broken. Electrical energy is then released.

The flowers in your garden are examples of stored chemical energy.

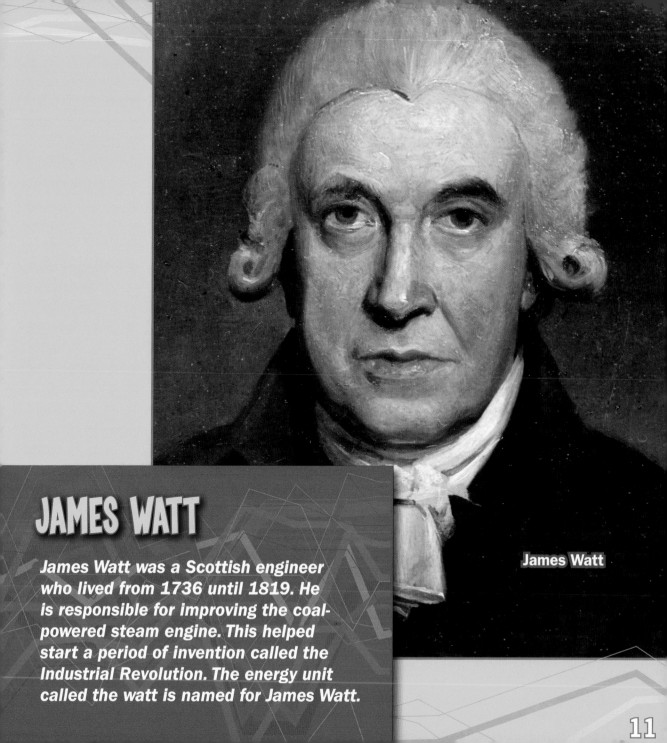

JAMES WATT

James Watt was a Scottish engineer who lived from 1736 until 1819. He is responsible for improving the coal-powered steam engine. This helped start a period of invention called the Industrial Revolution. The energy unit called the watt is named for James Watt.

James Watt

11

HOW DO BATTERIES WORK?

Batteries are stored chemical energy. Inside the battery, there are different chemicals stored in different parts of the battery. The battery's chemical energy is released when the positive and negative ends of the battery are connected to complete a **circuit**. A circuit is a complete path through which electrical energy flows.

Cars have batteries that power things like the lights, the radio, and the starter.

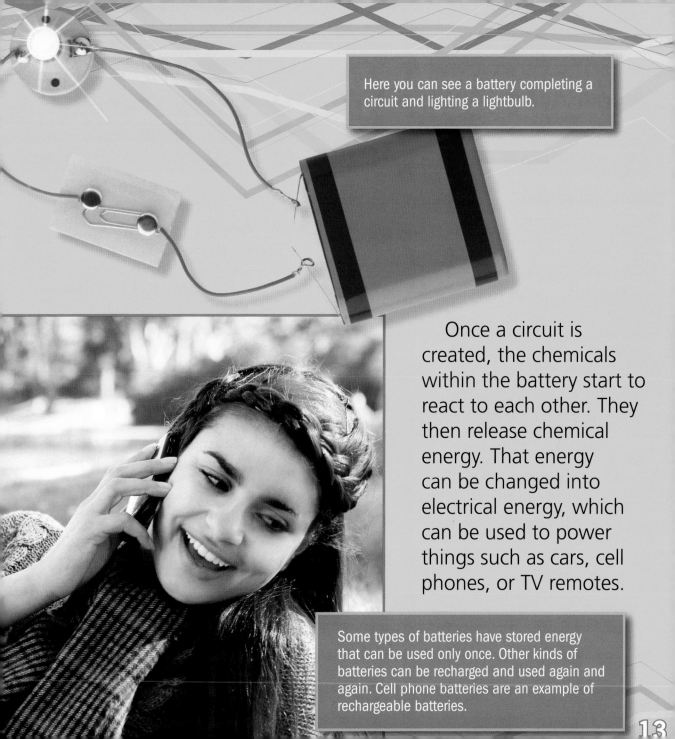

Here you can see a battery completing a circuit and lighting a lightbulb.

Once a circuit is created, the chemicals within the battery start to react to each other. They then release chemical energy. That energy can be changed into electrical energy, which can be used to power things such as cars, cell phones, or TV remotes.

Some types of batteries have stored energy that can be used only once. Other kinds of batteries can be recharged and used again and again. Cell phone batteries are an example of rechargeable batteries.

13

PLANTS AND CHEMICAL ENERGY

A carrot is an example of chemical energy stored in plants. A plant absorbs, or takes in, light energy from the Sun through its leaves. The plant transforms the light energy into chemical energy through **photosynthesis**. This is a process in which the plant uses sunlight, carbon dioxide, and water to produce food for itself.

A large peach has about 60 calories. Peaches are the fruit of the peach tree.

One carrot has about 30 calories, depending on its size. It is the root of the carrot plant.

The plant stores chemical energy in its leaves, stems, and roots. When we eat that plant or any other food, the amount of energy it gives us is measured in **calories**. Calories are the amount of energy in the chemical bonds between molecules that make up our food.

FASCINATING FOSSIL FUELS

Most cars and many houses are powered by fossil fuels. These energy sources, which include coal, oil, and natural gas, are found deep within the earth.

Fossil fuels took millions of years to form. As trees and other plants died, they sank to the bottom of oceans.

Fossil fuels got their name because they are made of the same kinds of plant life that became fossils.

As with other fossil fuels, oil must be drilled from deep under the ground using special machines, like these pump jacks.

They were covered over with layers of rock and sand. The trees and plants were **compressed** over millions of years until they formed fossil fuels.

When we burn fossil fuels, their stored chemical energy is converted, or changed, into mechanical energy to power our car engines or to run our power plants.

RELEASING CHEMICAL ENERGY

The scientific term combustion refers to the chemical reaction that happens when a fuel and air are mixed. When wood combusts, the chemical energy contained within the logs is released in the form of fire, which is both light energy and heat energy.

About 42 percent of the electricity in the United States is generated by coal-burning power plants.

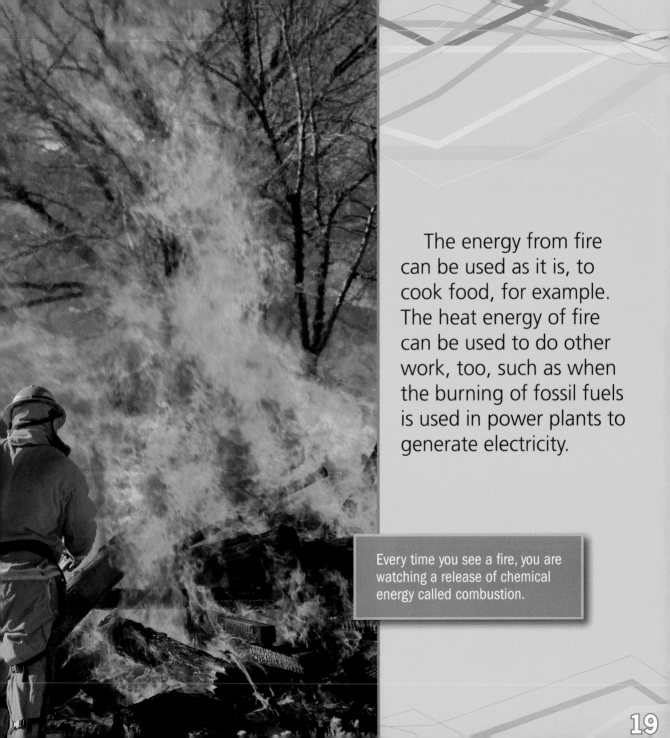

The energy from fire can be used as it is, to cook food, for example. The heat energy of fire can be used to do other work, too, such as when the burning of fossil fuels is used in power plants to generate electricity.

Every time you see a fire, you are watching a release of chemical energy called combustion.

CONVERTING CHEMICAL ENERGY

One of the most important rules of energy is that it cannot be created or destroyed, no matter what form it is converted into. Energy always exists, it just keeps being converted again and again.

When we convert energy, not all of the energy being converted will be transformed into the form we want to use.

In an incandescent lightbulb, like the one shown here, only about 10 percent of the energy it gives off is light energy. The other 90 percent is heat energy that goes unused.

Because we cannot use this energy, it is thought of as wasted energy. For instance, when electrical energy is converted to light energy in a lightbulb, there is heat energy given off, too. This heat is wasted energy.

Easy Bake

This toy uses the heat energy of a lightbulb that usually goes to waste to bake cakes and other treats!

CHEMICAL ENERGY EVERYWHERE

From the cars in the street to the batteries in your toys, chemical energy is everywhere in our world. The fossil fuels that contain the stored chemical energy we combust to power our world are **nonrenewable** sources of energy. That means that they will be used up someday.

Other sources we use for power, like **solar energy**, are **renewable**, meaning they can never be used up. They are an important, growing part of our world of energy.

Hybrid electric cars, like the ones shown here, are made to use less gasoline. Their owners can plug them in to be refueled instead of putting gas in them.

GLOSSARY

bond (BOND) To hold two things together.

calories (KA-luh-reez) Amounts of food that the body uses to keep working.

chemical (KEH-mih-kul) Matter that can be mixed with other matter to cause changes.

circuit (SER-ket) The complete path of an electric current.

compressed (kum-PRESD) Squeezed something into a smaller space.

fossil fuels (FO-sul FYOOLZ) Fuels, such as coal, natural gas, or gasoline, that were made from plants that died millions of years ago.

matter (MA-ter) Anything that has weight and takes up space.

molecules (MAH-lih-kyoolz) Two or more atoms joined together.

nonrenewable (non-ree-NOO-uh-bul) Not able to be replaced once used.

particles (PAR-tih-kulz) Small pieces of matter.

photosynthesis (foh-toh-SIN-thuh-sus) The way in which green plants make their own food from sunlight, water, and a gas called carbon dioxide.

reactions (ree-AK-shunz) Actions caused by things that have happened.

renewable (ree-NOO-uh-bul) Able to be replaced once it is used up.

solar energy (SOH-ler EH-nur-jee) Heat and light created by the Sun.

INDEX

C
circuit, 12–13

E
electricity, 4, 19

F
flames, 4

H
heat, 4, 21

K
kinds, 4

L
light, 4, 10

M
molecules, 6–7, 15

P
particles, 6

R
reaction(s), 4, 8, 18
rock, 6, 17

S
sound, 4
sources, 16, 22
space, 6
stomach, 4, 9
sunlight, 4, 14
system, 4

WEBSITES

Due to the changing nature of Internet links, PowerKids Press has developed an online list of websites related to the subject of this book. This site is updated regularly. Please use this link to access the list: www.powerkidslinks.com/enev/speed/